90 English Translations of the Famous Psalm 23 The LORD is my Shepherd

Compiled by Michael Dow

D1444452

90 English Translations of the Famous Psalm 23 The LORD is my Shepherd

The intention of this research to reprint the same verses from many different bibles and books is for teaching. It is the hope that this book will be used by individuals and groups to increase the faith of believers in the Coming of the Messiah, although Jesus said all we need is faith the size of a grain of mustard seed.

First Edition

ISBN 978-1-71678-955-7

Published by Lulu.com

Table of Contents

Table of Contents

Table of Contents

Preface

Psalm 23 is well loved by many. Some bibles have Psalm 10 as Psalm 9b so this Psalm is also called Psalm 22. There are 90 English translations of this passage in this book. In full disclosure, three Christian Bibles were not included because it did not say the word shepherd in the first line, but Directs me, Ruleth me, and Governeth me. The old English translations were not included since they may make things confusing due to their unusual spelling.

The Appendix of this book has a list of questions that you can answer by yourself or as a group to help explore your faith and build stronger bonds with others as you answer together.

Prologue

This is a Psalm of David. Enjoy the little differences among all of these translations and may your walk with the LORD be closer and deeper as you get to know him as a Shepherd and us as his sheep.

Hebrew Bible – Alter's Translation

The LORD is my shepherd,

I shall not want.

In grass meadows He makes me lie down,

by quiet waters guides me.

My life He brings back.

He leads me on pathways of justice

for His name's sake.

Though I walk in the vale of death's shadow,

I fear no harm,

for You are with me.

Your rod and Your staff –

it is they that console me.

You set out a table before me

in the face of my foes.

You moisten my head with oil,

my cup overflows.

Let but goodness and kindness pursue me

all the days of my life.

And I shall dwell in the house of the LORD

for many long days.

Hebrew Bible – JPS Hebrew-English TANAKH

The LORD is my shepherd;

I lack nothing.

He makes me lie down in green pastures;

He leads me to water in places of repose;

He renews my life;

He guides me in right paths

as befits His name.

Though I walk through a valley of deepest darkness,

I fear no harm, for You are with me;

Your rod and Your staff – they comfort me.

You spread a table for me in full view of my enemies;

You anoint my head with oil;

my drink is abundant.

Only goodness and steadfast love shall pursue me

all the days of my life,

and I shall dwell in the house of the LORD

for many long years.

Hebrew Bible – The Leeser Bible

The Lord is my shepherd, I shall not want.

In pastures of tender grass he causeth me to lie down:

beside still waters he leadeth me.

My soul he refresheth:

He guideth me in the tracks of righteousness

for the sake of his name.

Yea, though I walk through the valley of the shadow of death,

I will not fear evil; for thou art with me:

thy rod and thy staff – they indeed comfort me.

Thou prepares before me a table in the presence of my assailants;

thou anointest with oil my head:

my cup overfloweth.

Surely, only goodness and kindness shall follow me

all the days of my life:

And I shall dwell in the house of the Lord

to the utmost length of days.

Hebrew Bible – TANAKH The Holy Scriptures The New JPS Translation

The LORD is my shepherd;

I lack nothing.

He makes me lie down in green pastures;

He leads me to water in places of repose;

He renews my life;

He guides me in right paths

as befits His name.

Though I walk through a valley of deepest darkness,

I fear no harm, for You are with me;

Your rod and Your staff – they comfort me.

You spread a table for me in full view of my enemies;

You anoint my head with oil;

my drink is abundant.

Only goodness and steadfast love shall pursue me

all the days of my life,

and I shall dwell in the house of the LORD

for many long years.

5
American Standard Version

Jehovah is my shepherd; I shall not want.

He maketh me to lie down in green pastures;

He leadeth me beside still waters.

He restoreth my soul:

He guideth me in the paths of righteousness for his name's sake.

Yea, though I walk through the valley of the shadow of death,

I will fear no evil;

For thou art with me;

Thy rod and thy staff, they comfort me.

Thou prepares a table before me in the presence of mine enemies:

Thou hast anointed my head with oil;

My cup runneth over.

Surely goodness and lovingkindness shall follow me

all the days of my life;

And I shall dwell in the house of Jehovah for ever.

6
An American Translation

The LORD is my shepherd; I shall not want;

In green pastures he makes me lie down;

Beside refreshing waters he leads me.

He gives me new life;

He guides me in paths of righteousness for his name's sake.

Even though I walk in the darkest valley,

I fear no harm; for thou art with me;

Thy rod and thy staff – they comfort me.

Thou layest a table before me in the presence of my enemies;

Thou anointest my head with oil;

my cup overflows.

Surely goodness and kindness shall follow me

all the days of my life;

And I shall dwell in the house of the LORD

to an old age.

Amplified Bible

The LORD is my Shepherd [to feed, to guide and to shield me],

I shall not want.

He lets me lie down in green pastures;

He leads me beside the still and quiet waters.

He refreshes and restores my soul (life);

He leads me in the paths of righteousness for His name's sake.

Even though I walk through the [sunless] valley of the shadow of

death,

I fear no evil, for You are with me;

Your rod [to protect] and Your staff [to guide],

they comfort and console me.

You prepare a table before me in the presence of my enemies.

You have anointed and refreshed my head with oil;

My cup overflows.

Surely goodness and mercy and unfailing love shall follow me

all the days of my life,

And I shall dwell forever [throughout all my days]

in the house and in the presence of the LORD.

Amplified Bible, Classic Edition

THE LORD is my Shepherd [to feed, guide, and shield me],

I shall not lack.

He makes me lie down in [fresh, tender] green pastures;

He leads me beside the still and restful waters.

He refreshes and restores my life (my self);

He leads me in the paths of righteousness [uprightness and right

standing with Him – not for my earning it, but]

for His name's sake.

Yes, though I walk through the [deep, sunless] valley of the

shadow of death,

I will fear or dread no evil,

for You are with me;

Your rod [to protect] and Your staff [to guide],

they comfort me.

You prepare a table before me in the presence of my enemies.

You anoint my head with oil;

my [brimming] cup runs over.

Surely or only goodness, mercy, and unfailing love

shall follow me all the days of my life,

and through the length of my days

the house of the Lord [and His presence]

shall be my dwelling place.

Anchor Bible

Yahweh is my shepherd,

I shall not lack.

In green pastures he will make me lie down;

Near tranquil waters will he guide me,

to refresh my being.

He will lead me into luxuriant pastures,

as befits his name.

Even though I should walk

in the midst of total darkness,

I shall fear no danger

since you are with me.

Your rod and your staff –

Behold, they will lead me.

You prepare my table before me,

in front of my adversaries.

You generously anoint my head with oil,

my cup overflows.

Surely goodness and kindness will attend me,

all the days of my life;

And I shall dwell in the house of Yahweh

for days without end.

Berkeley Version

The LORD is my Shepherd;

I shall not lack;

He makes me to lie down in green pastures;

He leads me beside restful water;

He revives my soul.

He leads me in paths of righteousness for His name's sake.

Yes, though I walk through the valley of the shadow of death,

I will fear no ~~hard;~~ harm

for Thou art with me:

Thy rod and Thy staff, they comfort me.

Thou prepares a table before me in the presence of my adversaries;

Thou hast anointed my head with oil;

my cup runs over.

Surely, goodness and unfailing love shall follow me

all the days of my life

and I shall dwell in the house of the LORD forever.

11
The Bible in Living English

Jehovah is my shepherd;

I shall never have less than I need.

He has me lie down in green pastures;

he takes me to resting-places along the water.

He puts life back into me;

he leads me on trails that go right, for the sake of his name.

Even when I go in a valley of gloom

I will not be afraid of anything bad,

because you are with me;

Your club and staff,

they set my mind at rest.

You lay a table before me

in my foemen's presence;

You have lavished oil on my head,

my cup is full of refreshment.

I shall have nothing but kindness and friendliness following me

all my life,

and I shall stay at Jehovah's house for long years.

The Bible Translated in Simple English

The LORD is my shepherd.

I will not need anything.

He makes me lie down in green fields.

He leads me to waters where I can rest.

He gives me new life.

He is my guide to the right road.

He does this to (do what) his name (promises).

I will not be afraid when I walk through the valley of the shadow of

death.

This is because you (LORD) are with me.

Your rod and staff make me feel brave.

You prepare a table in front of me when my enemies are present.

You put oil on my head.

My cup is so full that it overflows.

I am sure that good and loving and kind things will follow me.

They will follow me all the days of my life.

I will always live in the house of the LORD.

Catholic Teen Bible

The LORD is my shepherd;

there is nothing I lack.

In green pastures he makes me lie down;

to still waters he leads me;

he restores my soul.

He guides me along right paths

for the sake of his name.

Even though I walk through the valley of the shadow of death,

I will fear no evil,

for you are with me;

your rod and your staff comfort me.

You set a table before me

in front of my enemies;

You anoint my head with oil;

my cup overflows.

Indeed, goodness and mercy will pursue me

all the days of my life;

I will dwell in the house of the LORD

for endless days.

Christian Community Bible

The Lord is my shepherd, I shall not want.

He makes me lie down in green pastures.

He leads me beside the still waters.

He restores my soul.

He guides me through the paths of righteousness

for his name's sake.

Although I walk through the valley of the shadow of death,

I fear no evil,

for you are beside me.

Your rod and your staff

are there to comfort me.

You prepare a table before me

in the presence of my foes.

You anoint my head with oil;

my cup is overflowing.

Goodness and kindness will follow me

all the days of my life,

I shall dwell in the house of the Lord

as long as I live.

Christian Standard Bible

The LORD is my shepherd;

I have what I need.

He lets me lie down in green pastures;

he leads me beside quiet waters.

He renews my life;

he leads me along the right paths

for his name's sake.

Even when I go through the darkest valley,

I fear no danger,

for you are with me;

your rod and your staff – they comfort me.

You prepare a table before me

in the presence of my enemies;

you anoint my head with oil;

my cup overflows.

Only goodness and faithful love will pursue me

all the days of my life,

and I will dwell in the house of the LORD

as long as I live.

The Clear Word

The Lord is my shepherd; I have everything I need.

He lets me lie down in green meadows.

He leads me beside quiet waters.

He restores the strength of my soul.

He guides me along paths of righteousness.

Even when I walk through a valley of frightful shadows facing

death,

I will fear no evil,

because you are with me.

Your rod and staff comfort me.

You spread out a banquet for me in the presence of my enemies.

You anoint my head with drops of oil.

My heart overflows with gratitude.

Your goodness and mercy will be with me every day of my life,

and I will live with the Lord in His house forever.

Common English Bible

The LORD is my shepherd.

I lack nothing.

He lets me rest in grassy meadows;

he leads me to restful waters;

he keeps me alive.

He guides me in proper paths

for the sake of his good name.

Even when I walk through the darkest valley,

I fear no danger because you are with me.

Your rod and your staff – they protect me.

You set a table for me right in front of my enemies.

You bathe my head in oil;

my cup is so full it spills over!

Yes, goodness and faithful love will pursue me

all the days of my life,

and I will live in the LORD's house

as long as I live.

Complete Jewish Bible

ADONAI is my shepherd; I lack nothing.

He has me lie down in grassy pastures,

he leads me by quiet water,

he restores my inner person.

He guides me in right paths

for the sake of his own name.

Even if I pass through death-dark ravines,

I will fear no disaster; for you are with me;

your rod and staff reassure me.

You prepare a table for me,

even as my enemies watch;

you anoint my head with oil

from an overflowing cup.

Goodness and grace will pursue me

every day of my life;

and I will live in the house of ADONAI

for years and years to come.

Confraternity Version

The Lord is my shepherd;

I shall not want.

In verdant pastures he gives me repose;

beside restful waters he leads me;

he refreshes my soul.

He guides me in right paths for his name's sake.

Even though I walk in the dark valley

I fear no evil;

for you are at my side

with your rod and your staff that give me courage.

You spread the table before me in the sight of my foes;

you anoint my head with oil;

my cup overflows.

Only goodness and kindness follow me all the days of my life;

and I shall dwell in the house of the Lord for years to come.

Contemporary English Version

You, LORD, are my shepherd.

I will never be in need.

You let me rest in fields of green grass.

You lead me to streams of peaceful water,

and you refresh my life.

You are true to your name,

and you lead me along the right paths.

I may walk through valleys as dark as death,

but I won't be afraid.

You are with me,

and your shepherd's rod makes me feel safe.

You treat me to a feast while my enemies watch.

You honor me as your guest,

and you fill my cup until it overflows.

Your kindness and love will always be with me

each day of my life,

and I will live forever in your house, LORD.

The CTS New Catholic Bible

The Lord is my shepherd;

there is nothing I shall want.

Fresh and green are the pastures where he gives me repose.

Near restful waters he leads me,

to revive my drooping spirit.

He guides me along the right path;

he is true to his name.

If I should walk in the valley of darkness

no evil would I fear.

You are there with your crook and your staff;

with these you give me comfort.

You have prepared a banquet for me in the sight of my foes.

My head you have anointed with oil;

my cup is overflowing.

Surely goodness and kindness shall follow me

all the days of my life.

In the Lord's own house shall I dwell for ever and ever.

Darby's Translation

Jehovah is my shepherd; I shall not want.

He maketh me to lie down in green pastures;

he leadeth me beside still waters.

He restoreth my soul;

he leadeth me in paths of righteousness for his name's sake.

Yea, though I walk through the valley of the shadow of death;

I will fear no evil:

for thou art with me;

thy rod and thy staff, they comfort me.

Thou prepares a table before me in the presence of mine enemies;

thou hast anointed my head with oil;

my cup runneth over.

Surely, goodness and loving-kindness shall follow me

all the days of my life;

and I will dwell in the house of Jehovah

for the length of the days.

23

EasyEnglish Bible

The LORD takes care of me,

like a shepherd with his sheep.

I have everything that I need.

He takes me to green fields where I can rest.

He leads me to streams of water where I can drink.

He gives me new strength in my life.

He is my guide to the right paths.

He does this to show that he is good.

I may walk through a valley that is as dark as death.

But I will not be afraid of any danger.

This is because you are with me, LORD.

Your stick and your shepherd's pole make me feel brave.

You prepare a big meal for me while my enemies watch.

You put olive oil on my head.

You bless me so much that my cup is completely full.

I am sure that you will always be good to me.

You will love me all the days of my life.

That will never change.

I will live in the LORD's house for as long as I live.

Easy to Read Version

The LORD is my shepherd.

I will always have everything I need.

He gives me green pastures to lie in.

He leads me by calm pools of water.

He restores my strength.

He leads me on right paths to show that he is good.

Even if I walk through a valley as dark as the grave,

I will not be afraid of any danger,

because you are with me.

Your rod and staff comfort me.

You prepared a meal for me in front of my enemies.

You welcomed me as an honored guest.

My cup is full and spilling over.

Your goodness and mercy will be with me all my life,

and I will live in the LORD's house a long, long time.

Emphasized Bible

Yahweh is my shepherd – I shall not want:

In pastures of tender grass he maketh me lie down.

Unto restful waters he leadeth me;

My life he restoreth,

He guideth me in right paths for the sake of his Name.

Yea though I walk through a valley death-shadowed

I will fear no harm for thou art with me,

Thy rod and thy staff they comfort me.

Thou spreadest before me a table in face of mine adversaries,

Thou hast anointed with oil my head,

My cup hath run over.

Surely goodness and lovingkindness will pursue me

all the days of my life,

And I shall dwell in the house of Yahweh evermore.

English Standard Version

The LORD is my shepherd; I shall not want.

He makes me lie down in green pastures.

He leads me beside still waters.

He restores my soul.

He leads me in paths of righteousness for his name's sake.

Even though I walk through the valley of the shadow of death,

I will fear no evil,

for you are with me;

your rod and your staff,

they comfort me.

You prepare a table before me in the presence of my enemies;

you anoint my head with oil;

my cup overflows.

Surely goodness and mercy shall follow me

all the days of my life,

and I shall dwell in the house of the LORD

forever.

Free Bible Version New Testament with Psalms

Since the Lord is my shepherd, I have everything I need.

He gives me rest in green fields.

He leads me towards quietly flowing streams.

He revives me.

He guides me along the right paths

because that's the kind of person he is.

Even when I walk through the valley dark as death,

I'm not afraid of any evil,

because you are right there with me;

your rod and your staff protect me.

You prepare a banquet for me before my enemies.

You honor me by anointing my head with oil.

My cup is so full it overflows!

I'm absolutely certain that your goodness and trustworthy love

will be with me all through my life,

and I will live in the house of the Lord forever.

God's Word

The LORD is my shepherd.

I am never in need.

He makes me lie down in green pastures.

He leads me beside peaceful waters.

He renews my soul.

He guides me along the paths of righteousness

for the sake of his name.

Even though I walk through the dark valley of death,

because you are with me, I fear no harm.

Your rod and your staff give me courage.

You prepare a banquet for me while my enemies watch.

You anoint my head with oil.

My cup overflows.

Certainly, goodness and mercy will stay close to me

all the days of my life,

and I will remain in the LORD's house for days without end.

Good News Bible

The LORD is my shepherd;

I have everything I need.

He lets me rest in fields of green grass

and leads me to quiet pools of fresh water.

He gives me new strength.

He guides me in the right paths,

as he has promised.

Even if I go through the deepest darkness,

I will not be afraid, LORD,

for you are with me.

Your shepherd's rod and staff protect me.

You prepare a banquet for me,

where all my enemies can see me;

you welcome me as an honored guest

and fill my cup to the brim.

I know that your goodness and love will be with me

all my life;

and your house will be my home as long as I live.

Holman Christian Standard Bible

The LORD is my shepherd;

there is nothing I lack.

He lets me lie down in green pastures;

He leads me beside quiet waters.

He renews my life;

He leads me along the right paths for His name's sake.

Even when I go through the darkest valley,

I fear no danger,

for You are with me;

Your rod and Your staff – they comfort me.

You prepare a table before me in the presence of my enemies;

You anoint my head with oil;

my cup overflows.

Only goodness and faithful love will pursue me

all the days of my life,

and I will dwell in the house of the LORD

as long as I live.

Holy Bible: containing the Old and New Testaments translated out of the Original Tongues

The LORD is my shepherd; I shall not want.

He maketh me to lie down in green pastures:

he leadeth me beside the still waters.

He restoreth my soul: he leadeth me in the paths of righteousness

for his name's sake.

Yea, though I walk through the valley of the shadow of death,

I will fear no evil:

for thou art with me;

thy rod and thy staff they comfort me.

Thou prepares a table before me in the presence of mine enemies:

thou anointest my head with oil;

my cup runneth over.

Surely goodness and mercy shall follow me

all the days of my life:

and I will dwell in the house of the LORD for ever.

The Holy Bible in the Language of Today

The LORD is my Shepherd – I have everything I need.

He makes me lie down in fresh green pastures

and leads me to water where I can rest.

He restores my life.

He leads me on paths of righteousness

for His name's sake.

Even though I walk in a very dark valley,

I fear no harm because You are with me;

Your rod and Your staff give me comfort.

You set a table before me right in front of my enemies.

You have anointed my head with oil;

my cup is running over.

Surely goodness and mercy will follow me all my life,

and I will live in the LORD's house forever.

Illuminated Bible

THE LORD is my shepherd; I shall not want.

He maketh me to lie down in green pastures:

he leadeth me beside the still waters.

He restoreth my soul:

he leadeth me in the paths of righteousness for his name's sake.

Yea, though I walk through the valley of the shadow of death,

I will fear no evil:

for thou art with me;

thy rod and thy staff they comfort me.

Thou prepares a table before me in the presence of mine enemies:

thou anointest my head with oil;

my cup runneth over.

Surely goodness and mercy shall follow me all the days of my life:

and I will dwell in the house of the LORD for ever.

Inspired Version

THE Lord is my shepherd; I shall not want.

He maketh me to lie down in green pastures;

he leadeth me beside the still waters.

He restoreth my soul;

he leadeth me in the paths of righteousness for his name's sake.

Yea, though I walk through the valley of the shadow of death,

I will fear no evil;

for thou art with me;

thy rod and thy staff comfort me.

Thou prepares a table before me in the presence of mine enemies;

thou anointest my head with oil;

my cup runneth over.

Surely goodness and mercy shall follow me all the days of my life;

And I will dwell in the house of the Lord for ever.

Interlinear Bible

Jehovah is my shepherd;

I shall not want.

He makes me lie down in green pastures;

He leads me to restful waters;

He restores my soul;

He guides me in paths of righteousness for His name's sake.

Yea, though I walk through the valley of the shadow of death,

I will fear no evil;

for You are with me;

Your rod and Your staff,

they comfort me.

You prepare a table for me before my enemies;

You anoint my head with oil;

my cup runs over.

Surely, goodness and mercy shall follow me all the days of my life;

and I shall dwell in the house of Jehovah

for as long as my days.

International Children's Bible

The Lord is my shepherd.

I have everything I need.

He gives me rest in green pastures.

He leads me to calm water.

He gives me new strength.

For the good of his name,

he leads me on paths that are right.

Even if I walk through a very dark valley,

I will not be afraid because you are with me.

Your rod and your walking stick comfort me.

You prepare a meal for me in front of my enemies.

You pour oil on my head.

You give me more that I can hold.

Surely your goodness and love will be with me

all my life.

And I will live in the house of the Lord forever.

The Jubilee Bible

The LORD is my shepherd; I shall not want.

He makes me to lie down in green pastures;

he leads me beside the still waters.

He restores my soul:

he leads me in the paths of righteousness for his name's sake.

Yea, though I walk through the valley of the shadow of death,

I will fear no evil:

for thou art with me;

thy rod and thy staff shall comfort me.

Thou shalt prepare a table before me in the presence of my enemies;

thou hast anointed my head with oil;

my cup is running over.

Surely goodness and mercy shall follow me all the days of my life:

and I will rest in the house of the LORD for ever.

King James Version

The LORD is my shepherd; I shall not want.

He maketh me to lie down in green pastures:

he leadeth me beside the still waters.

He restoreth my soul:

he leadeth me in the paths of righteousness for his name's sake.

Yea, though I walk through the valley of the shadow of death,

I will fear no evil:

for thou art with me;

thy rod and thy staff they comfort me.

Thou prepares a table before me in the presence of mine enemies:

thou anointest my head with oil;

my cup runneth over.

Surely goodness and mercy shall follow me all the days of my life:

And I will dwell in the house of the LORD for ever.

King James Version
Divine Name Edition

Jehovah is my shepherd; I shall not want.

He maketh me to lie down in green pastures:

he leadeth me beside the still waters.

He restoreth my soul:

he leadeth me in the paths of righteousness for his name's sake.

Yea, though I walk through the valley of the shadow of death,

I will fear no evil:

for thou art with me;

thy rod and thy staff they comfort me.

Thou prepares a table before me in the presence of mine enemies:

thou anointest my head with oil;

my cup runneth over.

Surely goodness and mercy shall follow me all the days of my life:

And I will dwell in the house of Jehovah for ever.

Knox's Translation

The Lord is my shepherd; how can I lack anything?

He gives me a resting-place where there is green pasture,

leads me out to the cool water's brink,

refreshed and content.

As in honour pledged, by sure paths he leads me;

dark be the valley about my path,

hurt I fear none while he is with me;

thy rod, thy crook are my comfort.

Envious my foes watch, while thou dost spread a banquet for me;

richly thou dost anoint my head with oil,

well filled my cup.

All my life thy loving favour pursues me;

through the long years the Lord's house shall be my dwelling-place.

Lamsa's Translation

The LORD is my shepherd; I shall not want.

He makes me to rest in green pastures;

he leads me beside still waters.

He restores my soul.

He leads me in the paths of righteousness for his name's sake.

Yea, though I walk through the valley of the shadow of death,

I will fear no evil;

for thou art with me;

thy rod and thy staff they comfort me.

Thou prepares a table before me in the presence of mine enemies;

thou anointest my head with oil;

my cup runneth over.

Surely thy goodness and mercy shall follow me

all the days of my life;

and I shall dwell in the house of the LORD for ever.

The Lexham English Bible

Yahweh is my shepherd;

I will not lack for anything.

In grassy pastures he makes me lie down;

by quiet waters he leads me.

He restores my life.

He leads me in correct paths for the sake of his name.

Even when I walk in a dark valley,

I fear no evil

because you are with me.

Your rod and your staff, they comfort me.

You prepare before me a table in the presence of my oppressors.

You anoint my head with oil;

my cup is overflowing.

Surely goodness and loyal love will pursue me

all the days of my life,

and I will stay in the house of Yahweh

for a very long time.

The Literal Standard Version

YHWH [is] my shepherd, I do not lack.

He causes me to lie down in pastures of tender grass,

He leads me by quiet waters.

He refreshes my soul,

He leads me in paths of righteousness

For His Name's sake;

Also – when I walk in a valley of death-shade,

I fear no evil, for You [are] with me,

Your rod and Your staff – they comfort me.

You arrange a table before me,

In front of my adversaries,

You have anointed my head with oil,

My cup is full!

Surely goodness and kindness pursue me

All the days of my life,

And my dwelling [is] in the house of YHWH,

For [the] length of [my] days!

The Living Bible

Because the Lord is my Shepherd, I have everything I need!

He lets me rest in the meadow grass

and leads me beside the quiet streams.

He restores my failing health.

He helps me do what honors him the most.

Even when walking through the dark valley of death

I will not be afraid, for you are close beside me,

guarding, guiding all the way.

You provide delicious food for me in the presence of my enemies.

You have welcomed me as your guest;

blessings overflow!

Your goodness and unfailing kindness shall be with me

all of my life,

and afterwards I will live with you forever in your home.

The Message

GOD, my shepherd!

I don't need a thing.

You have bedded me down in lush meadows,

you find me quiet pools to drink from.

True to your word,

you let me catch my breath

and send me in the right direction.

Even when the way goes through Death Valley,

I'm not afraid when you walk at my side.

Your trusty shepherd's crook makes me feel secure.

You serve me a six-course dinner

right in front of my enemies.

You revive my drooping head;

my cup brims with blessing.

Your beauty and love chase after me every day of my life.

I'm back home in the house of GOD

for the rest of my life.

Metrical Psalms 1650

The Lord's my shepherd, I'll not want.

He makes me down to lie

In pastures green:

he leadeth me the quiet waters by.

My soul he doth restore again;

and me to walk doth make

Within the paths of righteousness,

ev'n for his own name's sake.

Yea, though I walk in death's dark vale,

yet will I fear none ill:

For thou art with me;

and thy rod and staff me comfort still.

My table thou hast furnished in presence of my foes;

My head thou dost with oil anoint,

and my cup overflows.

Goodness and mercy all my life shall surely follow me:

And in God's house for evermore my dwelling-place shall be.

Modern English Version

The LORD is my shepherd; I shall not want.

He makes me lie down in green pastures;

He leads me beside still waters.

He restores my soul;

He leads me in paths of righteousness for His name's sake.

Even though I walk through the valley of the shadow of death,

I will fear no evil;

for You are with me;

Your rod and Your staff,

they comfort me.

You prepare a table before me in the presence of my enemies;

You anoint my head with oil;

my cup runs over.

Surely goodness and mercy shall follow me

all the days of my life,

and I will dwell in the house of the LORD forever.

Moffatt's Translation

The Eternal shepherds me, I lack for nothing;

he makes me lie in meadows green,

he leads me to refreshing streams,

he revives life in me.

He guides me by true paths,

as he himself is true.

My road may run through a glen of doom,

but I fear no harm, for thou art beside me;

thy club, thy staff – they give me courage.

Thou art my host, spreading a feast for me,

while my foes have to look on!

Thou hast poured oil upon my head,

my cup is brimming over;

yes, and all through my life

Goodness and Kindness wait on me,

the Eternal's guest within his household evermore.

New American Bible

The LORD is my shepherd;

there is nothing I lack.

In green pastures you let me graze;

to safe waters you lead me;

you restore my strength.

You guide me along the right path

for the sake of your name.

Even when I walk through a dark valley,

I fear no harm for you are at my side;

your rod and staff give me courage.

You set a table before me as my enemies watch;

You anoint my head with oil;

my cup overflows.

Only goodness and love will pursue me

all the days of my life;

I will dwell in the house of the LORD

for years to come.

New American Bible
Revised Edition

The LORD is my shepherd;

there is nothing I lack.

In green pastures he makes me lie down;

to still waters he leads me;

he restores my soul.

He guides me along right paths

for the sake of his name.

Even though I walk through the valley of the shadow of death,

I will fear no evil,

for you are with me;

your rod and your staff comfort me.

You set a table before me in front of my enemies;

You anoint my head with oil;

my cup overflows.

Indeed, goodness and mercy will pursue me

all the days of my life;

I will dwell in the house of the LORD

for endless days.

New American Standard Bible

The LORD is my shepherd,

I shall not want.

He makes me lie down in green pastures;

He leads me beside quiet waters.

He restores my soul;

He guides me in the paths of righteousness

For His name's sake.

Even though I walk through the valley of the shadow of death,

I fear no evil, for You are with me;

Your rod and Your staff, they comfort me.

You prepare a table before me in the presence of my enemies;

You have anointed my head with oil;

My cup overflows.

Surely goodness and lovingkindness will follow me

all the days of my life,

And I will dwell in the house of the LORD forever.

New Berkeley Version

The LORD is my Shepherd; I shall not lack;

He makes me to lie down in green pastures;

He leads me beside restful water;

He revives my soul.

He leads me in paths of righteousness for His name's sake.

Yes, though I walk through the valley of the shadow of death,

I will fear no harm; for Thou art with me:

Thy rod and Thy staff, they comfort me.

Thou prepares a table before me in the presence of my adversaries;

Thou hast anointed my head with oil;

my cup runs over.

Surely, goodness and unfailing love shall follow me

all the days of my life

and I shall dwell in the house of the LORD forever.

New Catholic Bible
St. Joseph Edition

The LORD is my shepherd;

there is nothing I shall lack.

He makes me lie down in green pastures;

he leads me to tranquil streams.

He restores my soul,

guiding me in paths of righteousness

so that his name may be glorified.

Even though I wander through the valley of the shadow of death,

I will fear no evil,

for you are at my side,

with your rod and your staff that comfort me.

You spread a table for me in the presence of my enemies.

You anoint my head with oil;

my cup overflows.

Only goodness and kindness will follow me

all the days of my life,

and I will dwell in the house of the LORD forever and ever.

New Century Version

The LORD is my shepherd;

I have everything I need.

He lets me rest in green pastures.

He leads me to calm water.

He gives me new strength.

He leads me on paths that are right for the good of his name.

Even if I walk through a very dark valley,

I will not be afraid,

because you are with me.

Your rod and your walking stick comfort me.

You prepare a meal for me in front of my enemies.

You pour oil on my head;

you fill my cup to overflowing.

Surely your goodness and love will be with me all my life,

and I will live in the house of the LORD forever.

New Community Bible

The LORD is my shepherd, what more do I need?

In green pastures he lets me rest.

To quiet streams of water he leads me,

and revives my failing spirit.

He leads me along the right paths ~~every~~ *eve* true to his name.

Even though I walk through the valley of the shadows of death,

no harm would I fear, for you are there by my side.

With your rod and your staff you give me comfort.

You prepare a banquet for me in the presence of my foes.

You anoint my head with oil;

my cup is overflowing.

Only goodness and kindness will follow me

all the days of my life,

I shall dwell in the house of the LORD

for ever and ever.

New English Bible

The LORD is my shepherd; I shall want nothing.

He makes me lie down in green pastures,

and leads me beside the waters of peace;

he renews life within me,

and for his name's sake guides me in the right path.

Even though I walk through a valley dark as death

I fear no evil, for thou art with me,

thy staff and thy crook are my comfort.

Thou spreadest a table for me in the sight of my enemies;

Thou hast richly bathed my head with oil,

and my cup runs over.

Goodness and love unfailing,

these will follow me all the days of my life,

and I shall dwell in the house of the LORD

my whole life long.

New English Translation

The LORD is my shepherd,

I lack nothing.

He takes me to lush pastures,

he leads me to refreshing water.

He restores my strength.

He leads me down the right paths for the sake of his reputation.

Even when I must walk through the darkest valley,

I fear no danger,

for you are with me;

your rod and your staff reassure me.

You prepare a feast before me in plain sight of my enemies,

You refresh my head with oil;

my cup is completely full.

Surely your goodness and faithfulness will pursue me all my days,

and I will live in the LORD's house for the rest of my life.

New Illuminated Holy Bible

The LORD is my shepherd; I shall not want.

He maketh me to lie down in green pastures:

he leadeth me beside the still waters.

He restoreth my soul:

he leadeth me in the paths of righteousness for his name's sake.

Yea, though I walk through the valley of the shadow of death,

I will fear no evil:

for thou art with me;

thy rod and thy staff they comfort me.

Thou prepares a table before me in the presence of mine enemies:

thou anointest my head with oil;

my cup runneth over.

Surely goodness and mercy shall follow me all the days of my life:

And I will dwell in the house of the LORD for ever.

New International Reader's Version

The LORD is my shepherd. He gives me everything I need.

He lets me lie down in fields of green grass.

He leads me beside quiet waters.

He gives me new strength.

He guides me in the right paths for the honor of his name.

Even though I walk through the darkest valley,

I will not be afraid.

You are with me.

Your shepherd's rod and staff comfort me.

You prepare a feast for me right in front of my enemies.

You pour oil on my head.

My cup runs over.

I am sure that your goodness and love will follow me

all the days of my life.

And I will live in the house of the LORD forever.

New International Version

The LORD is my shepherd, I shall not be in want.

He makes me lie down in green pastures,

he leads me beside quiet waters,

he restores my soul.

He guides me in paths of righteousness for his name's sake.

Even though I walk through the valley of the shadow of death,

I will fear no evil,

for you are with me;

your rod and your staff,

they comfort me.

You prepare a table before me in the presence of my enemies.

You anoint my head with oil;

my cup overflows.

Surely goodness and love will follow me

all the days of my life,

and I will dwell in the house of the LORD forever.

New International Version Inclusive Language Edition

The LORD is my shepherd, I shall not be in want.

He makes me lie down in green pastures,

he leads me beside quiet waters,

he restores my soul.

He guides me in paths of righteousness for his name's sake.

Even though I walk through the valley of the shadow of death,

I will fear no evil,

for you are with me;

your rod and your staff,

they comfort me.

You prepare a table before me in the presence of my enemies.

You anoint my head with oil;

my cup overflows.

Surely goodness and love will follow me

all the days of my life,

and I will dwell in the house of the LORD forever.

New Jerusalem Bible

Yahweh is my shepherd, I lack nothing.

In grassy meadows he lets me lie.

By tranquil streams he leads me to restore my spirit.

He guides me in paths of saving justice as befits his name.

Even were I to walk in a ravine as dark as death

I should fear no danger, for you are at my side.

Your staff and your crook are there to soothe me.

You prepare a table for me under the eyes of my enemies;

you anoint my head with oil;

my cup brims over.

Kindness and faithful love pursue me every day of my life.

I make my home in the house of Yahweh for all time to come.

New King James Version

The LORD is my shepherd;

I shall not want.

He makes me to lie down in green pastures;

He leads me beside the still waters.

He restores my soul;

He leads me in the paths of righteousness

For His name's sake.

Yea, though I walk through the valley of the shadow of death,

I will fear no evil;

For You are with me;

Your rod and Your staff, they comfort me.

You prepare a table before me in the presence of my enemies;

You anoint my head with oil;

My cup runs over.

Surely goodness and mercy shall follow me

All the days of my life;

And I will dwell in the house of the LORD

Forever.

New Life Version

The Lord is my Shepherd.

I will have everything I need.

He lets me rest in fields of green grass.

He leads me beside the quiet waters.

He makes me strong again.

He leads me in the way of living right with Himself

which brings honor to His name.

Yes, even if I walk through the valley of the shadow of death,

I will not be afraid of anything,

because You are with me.

You have a walking stick with which to guide and one with which to

help.

These comfort me.

You are making a table of food ready for me

in front of those who hate me.

You have poured oil on my head.

I have everything I need.

For sure, You will give me goodness and loving-kindness

all the days of my life.

Then I will live with You in Your house forever.

New Living Translation

The LORD is my shepherd;
I have everything I need.
He lets me rest in green meadows;
he leads me beside peaceful streams.
He renews my strength.
He guides me along right paths,
bringing honor to his name.

Even when I walk through the dark valley of death,
I will not be afraid,
for you are close beside me.
Your rod and your staff protect and comfort me.

You prepare a feast for me in the presence of my enemies.
You welcome me as a guest,
anointing my head with oil.
My cup overflows with blessings.
Surely goodness and unfailing love will pursue me
all the days of my life,
and I will live in the house of the LORD forever.

New Messianic Version Bible

Yehovah Ro'i [Messiah Pre-Incarnate My shepherd];

I shall not lack.

He makes me to lie down in green pastures:

he leads me beside the still waters.

He restores my soul:

he leads me in the paths of righteousness for his name's sake.

Yea, though I walk through the valley of the shadow of death,

I will fear no evil:

for you [are] with me;

your rod and your staff they comfort me.

You prepare a table before me in the presence of mine enemies:

you anoint my head with oil;

my cup runs over.

Surely goodness and mercy shall follow me

all the days of my life:

and I will dwell in the house of the LORD-Yehovah [Messiah Pre-Incarnate] forever.

New Revised Standard Version

The LORD is my shepherd, I shall not want.

He makes me lie down in green pastures;

he leads me beside still waters;

he restores my soul.

He leads me in right paths for his name's sake.

Even though I walk through the darkest valley,

I fear no evil;

for you are with me;

your rod and your staff – they comfort me.

You prepare a table before me in the presence of my enemies;

you anoint my head with oil;

my cup overflows.

Surely goodness and mercy shall follow me

all the days of my life,

and I shall dwell in the house of the LORD

my whole life long.

New World Translation of the Holy Scriptures

Jehovah is my Shepherd.

I will lack nothing.

In grassy pastures he makes me lie down;

He leads me to well-watered resting places.

He refreshes me.

He leads me in the paths of righteousness for the sake of his name.

Though I walk in the valley of deep shadow,

I fear no harm,

For you are with me;

Your rod and your staff reassure me.

You prepare a table for me before my enemies.

You refresh my head with oil;

My cup is well-filled.

Surely goodness and loyal love will pursue me

all the days of my life,

And I will dwell in the house of Jehovah for all my days.

Open English Bible

The LORD is my shepherd: I am never in need.

He lays me down in green pastures.

He gently leads me to waters of rest,

he refreshes my life.

He guides me along paths that are straight,

true to his name.

And when my way lies through a valley of gloom,

I fear no evil, for you are with me.

Your rod and your staff comfort me.

You spread a table for me in face of my foes;

With oil you anoint my head,

and my cup runs over.

Surely goodness and love will pursue me –

all the days of my life.

In the house of the LORD I will live

through the length of the days.

Orthodox Jewish Bible

Hashem is my Ro'eh (Shepherd);

I shall not lack.

He maketh me to lie down in green pastures;

He leadeth me beside the mei menuchot (tranquil waters).

He restoreth my nefesh;

He guideth me in the paths of tzedek I'ma'an Shmo (righteousness

for the sake of His Name).

Yea, though I walk through the Gey Tzalmavet (Valley of the

Shadow of Death),

I will fear no rah (evil);

for Thou art with me;

Thy shevet (rod) and Thy staff they comfort me.

Thou prepares a shulchan before me in the presence of mine

enemies:

Thou anointest my head with shemen (olive oil);

my kos runneth over.

Surely tov and chesed shall follow me kol y'mei chaiyyai (all the

days of my life):

and I will dwell in the Bais Hashem l'orech yamim (for length of

days, whole life long, forever).

The Passion Translation

The Lord is my best friend and my shepherd.

I always have more than enough.

He offers a resting place for me in his luxurious love.

His tracks take me to an oasis of peace, the quiet brook of bliss.

That's where he restores and revives my life.

He opens before me pathways to God's pleasure

and leads me along in his footsteps of righteousness

so that I can bring honor to his name.

Lord, even when your path takes me through the valley of the

deepest darkness,

fear will never conquer me, for you already have!

You remain close to me and lead me through it all the way.

Your authority is my strength and my ~~pace~~. peace

The comfort of your love takes away my fear.

I'll never be lonely, for you are near.

You become my delicious feast even when my enemies dare to fight.

You anoint me with the fragrance of your Holy Spirit;

You give me all I can drink of you until my heart overflows.

So why would I fear the future?

For your goodness and love pursue me all the days of my life.

Then afterward, when my life is through,

I'll return to your glorious presence to be forever with you!

Purver's Translation

The Lord is my Shepherd, I do not want

He makes me lie down in Pastures of fresh Grass,

leads me by still Waters,

He restores my Soul,

guides me in the Roads of Righteousness, for his Name's sake

Nay though I go through the Valley of the Shadow of Death,

I fear no Ill,

since thou art with me,

whose Rod and Staff comfort me.

Thou furnisheth a Table for my Presence before my Adversaries,

maketh my Head wet with Oil,

my Cup is quite full

Certainly Goodness and Kindness will follow me all the Days of my

Life,

and I shall rest in the House of the Lord a long Time.

Revised English Bible

The LORD is my shepherd;

I lack for nothing.

He makes me lie down in green pastures,

he leads me to water where I may rest;

he revives my spirit;

for his name's sake he guides me in the right paths.

Even were I to walk through a valley of deepest darkness

I should fear no harm, for you are with me;

Your shepherd's staff and crook afford me comfort.

You spread a table for me in the presence of my enemies;

You have richly anointed my head with oil,

and my cup brims over.

Goodness and love unfailing will follow me

all the days of my life,

and I shall dwell in the house of the LORD

throughout the years to come.

Revised New Jerusalem Bible

The LORD is my shepherd;

there is nothing I shall want.

Fresh and green are the pastures

where he gives me repose.

Near restful waters he leads me;

he revives my soul.

He guides me along the right path,

for the sake of his name.

Though I should walk in the valley of the shadow of death,

no evil would I fear, for you are with me.

Your crook and your staff will give me comfort.

You have prepared a table before me

in the sight of my foes.

My head you have anointed with oil;

my cup is overflowing.

Surely goodness and mercy shall follow me

all the days of my life.

In the LORD's own house shall I dwell

for the length of days unending.

Revised Standard Version

The LORD is my shepherd, I shall not want;

he makes me lie down in green pastures.

He leads me beside still waters;

he restores my soul.

He leads me in paths of righteousness for his name's sake.

Even though I walk through the valley of the shadow of death,

I fear no evil;

for thou art with me;

thy rod and thy staff,

they comfort me.

Thou prepares a table before me in the presence of my enemies;

thou anointest my head with oil,

my cup overflows.

Surely goodness and mercy shall follow me

all the days of my life;

and I shall dwell in the house of the LORD

for ever.

Revised Version

The LORD is my shepherd; I shall not want.

He maketh me to lie down in green pastures:

He leadeth me beside the still waters.

He restoreth my soul:

He guideth me in the paths of righteousness for his name's sake.

Yea, though I walk through the valley of the shadow of death,

I will fear no evil; for thou art with me:

Thy rod and thy staff, they comfort me.

Thou prepares a table before me in the presence of mine enemies:

Thou hast anointed my head with oil;

my cup runneth over.

Surely goodness and mercy shall follow me

all the days of my life:

And I will dwell in the house of the LORD for ever.

Scofield Reference Edition

The LORD is my shepherd; I shall not want.

He maketh me to lie down in green pastures:

he leadeth me beside the still waters.

He restoreth my soul:

he leadeth me in the paths of righteousness for his name's sake.

Yea, though I walk through the valley of the shadow of death,

I will fear no evil: for thou art with me;

thy rod and thy staff they comfort me.

Thou prepares a table before me in the presence of mine enemies:

thou anointest my head with oil;

my cup runneth over.

Surely goodness and mercy shall follow me all the days of my life:

and I will dwell in the house of the LORD for ever.

The Scriptures

YHWH is my shepherd;

I do not lack.

He makes me to lie down in green pastures;

He leads me beside still waters.

He turns back my being;

He leads me in paths of righteousness

For His Name's sake.

When I walk through the valley of the shadow of death,

I fear no evil.

For You are with me;

Your rod and Your staff, they comfort me.

You spread before me a table in the face of my enemies;

You have anointed my head with oil;

My cup runs over.

Only goodness and loving-commitment follow me

All the days of my life;

And I shall dwell in the House of YHWH,

To the length of days!

The Septuagint – Brenton's Translation

The Lord tends me as a shepherd,

And I shall want nothing.

In a place of green grass, there he has made me dwell:

He has nourished me by the water of rest.

He has restored my soul:

He has guided me into the paths of righteousness,

for his name's sake.

Yea, even if I should walk in the midst of the shadow of death,

I will not be afraid of evils:

for thou art with me;

thy rod and thy staff, these have comforted me.

Thou hast prepared a table before me

in presence of them that afflict me:

thou hast thoroughly anointed my head with oil;

and thy cup cheers me like the best wine.

Thy mercy also shall follow me all the days of my life:

and my dwelling shall be in the house of the Lord

for a very long time.

The Septuagint –
The Lexham English Septuagint

The Lord shepherds me,

and nothing will be lacking for me.

In a place of tender grass, there he causes me to dwell.

At a river of rest he nourishes me.

He turns around my soul.

He leads me in paths of righteousness on account of His name.

For even if I should go in the middle of the shadow of death,

I will not fear evil things, because you are with me.

Your rod and your staff, they exhort me.

You prepare before me a table opposite those who afflict me.

You anoint my head with olive oil.

And your drinking cup is satisfying as the best.

Your mercy will pursue me all the days of my life,

and my dwelling will be in the house of the Lord

for the length of days.

The Septuagint –
The New English Translation of the Septuagint

The Lord shepherds me, and I shall lack nothing.

In a verdant place, there he made me encamp;

by water of rest he reared me;

my soul he restored.

He led me into paths of righteousness for his name's sake.

For even if I walk in the midst of death's shadow,

I will not fear evil, because you are with me;

your rod and your staff – they comforted me.

You prepared a table before me over against those that afflict me;

you anointed my head with oil,

and your cup was supremely intoxicating.

And your mercy shall pursue me all the days of my life,

and my residing in the Lord's house is for length of days.

The Septuagint – Orthodox Study Bible

The Lord is my shepherd; I shall not want.

He makes me to lie down in green pastures;

He leads me beside the still waters.

He restores my soul;

He leads me in the paths of righteousness

For His name's sake.

Yea, though I walk through the valley of the shadow of death,

I will fear no evil, for You are with me;

Your rod and Your staff, they comfort me.

You prepare a table before me in the presence of my enemies;

You anoint my head with oil;

My cup runs over.

Surely goodness and mercy shall follow me

All the days of my life;

And I will dwell in the house of the Lord to the end of my days.

J. E. Smith's Translation

Jehovah my shepherd, and I shall not want.

He will cause me to lie down in pastures of tender grass:

he will lead me to the water of rest.

He will turn back my soul:

he will guide me into the tracks of justice for sake of his name.

Also if I shall go into the valley of the shadow of death,

I shall not be afraid of evil, for thou art with me;

thy rod and thy staff they will comfort me.

Thou wilt set in order a table before me in front of mine enemies:

thou madest fat mine head with oil; my cup being satisfied with

drink.

Surely goodness and mercy shall pursue me all the days of my life:

And I dwelt in the house of Jehovah to the length of days.

Third Millennium Bible

The LORD is my shepherd;

I shall not want.

He maketh me to lie down in green pastures;

He leadeth me beside the still waters.

He restoreth my soul;

He leadeth me in the paths of righteousness for His name's sake.

Yea, though I walk through the valley of the shadow of death,

I will fear no evil;

for Thou art with me;

Thy rod and Thy staff, they comfort me.

Thou prepares a table before me in the presence of mine enemies;

Thou anointest my head with oil;

my cup runneth over.

Surely goodness and mercy shall follow me

all the days of my life;

and I will dwell in the house of the LORD for ever.

Tree of Life Version

ADONAI is my shepherd, I shall not want.

He makes me lie down in green pastures.

He leads me beside still waters.

He restores my soul.

He guides me in paths of righteousness for His Name's sake.

Even though I walk through the valley of the shadow of death,

I will fear no evil, for You are with me:

Your rod and Your staff comfort me.

You prepare a table before me in the presence of my enemies.

You have anointed my head with oil,

my cup overflows.

Surely goodness and mercy will follow me all the days of my life,

and I will dwell in the House of ADONAI forever.

The Voice Bible

The Eternal is my shepherd,

He cares for me always.

He provides me rest in rich, green fields

beside streams of refreshing water.

He soothes my fears;

He makes me whole again,

steering me off worn, hard paths

to roads where truth and righteousness echo His name.

Even in the unending shadows of death's darkness,

I am not overcome by fear.

Because You are with me in those dark moments,

near with Your protection and guidance,

I am comforted.

You spread out a table before me,

provisions in the midst of attack from my enemies;

You care for all my needs,

Anointing my head with soothing, fragrant oil,

filling my cup again and again with Your grace.

Certainly Your faithful protection and loving provision

will pursue me where I go, always, everywhere.

I will always be with the Eternal, in Your house forever.

Webster Bible of 1833

The LORD is my shepherd; I shall not want.

He maketh me to lie down in green pastures:

he leadeth me beside the still waters.

He restoreth my soul:

he leadeth me in the paths of righteousness for his name's sake.

Yes, though I walk through the valley of the shades of death,

I will fear no evil:

for thou art with me;

thy rod and thy staff they comfort me.

Thou prepares a table before me in the presence of my enemies:

thou anointest my head with oil;

my cup runneth over.

Surely goodness and mercy shall follow me all the days of my life:

and I will dwell in the house of the LORD for ever.

World English Bible

Yahweh is my shepherd: I shall lack nothing.

He makes me lie down in green pastures.

He leads me beside still waters.

He restores my soul.

He guides me in the paths of righteousness for his name's sake.

Even though I walk through the valley of the shadow of death,

I will fear no evil,

for you are with me.

Your rod and your staff, they comfort me.

You prepare a table before me in the presence of my enemies.

You anoint my head with oil.

My cup runs over.

Surely goodness and loving kindness shall follow me

all the days of my life,

and I will dwell in Yahweh's house forever.

World Messianic Bible

The LORD is my shepherd;

I shall lack nothing.

He makes me lie down in green pastures.

He leads me beside still waters.

He restores my soul.

He guides me in the paths of righteousness for his name's sake.

Even though I walk through the valley of the shadow of death,

I will fear no evil,

for you are with me.

Your rod and your staff,

they comfort me.

You prepare a table before me in the presence of my enemies.

You anoint my head with oil.

My cup runs over.

Surely goodness and loving kindness shall follow me

all the days of my life,

and I will dwell in the LORD's house forever.

Young's Literal Translation

Jehovah [is] my shepherd,

I do not lack,

In pastures of tender grass He causeth me to lie down,

By quiet waters He doth lead me.

My soul He refresheth,

He leadeth me in the paths of righteousness,

For His name's sake,

Also – when I walk in a valley of death-shade,

I fear no evil,

for Thou [art] with me,

Thy rod and Thy staff – they comfort me.

Thou arranges before me a table,

Over-against my adversaries,

Thou hast anointed with oil my head,

My cup is full!

Only – goodness and kindness pursue me,

All the days of my life,

And my dwelling [is] in the house of Jehovah,

For a length of days!

Epilogue

In case anyone was interested in my opinion about the best translation, I think it would be the Amplified Bible.

Appendix

Questions to Ponder Individually or as a Group

What are some basic things shepherds are responsible to do?

Why is the LORD compared to a Shepherd in the scriptures?

Can you see the LORD as a shepherd in your life?

Who in the bible has been compared to sheep?

Is there anything in your life that you are in true need of now?

What are the green pastures in your life?

How does the LORD make you lie down in green pastures?

How does the LORD lead you?

What are refreshing waters to you?

When in the past has the LORD refreshed your soul?

What did God use in your life to refresh you?

What are paths of righteousness that the LORD has led you down?

Have you ever noticed when the LORD was leading you to do the
right thing, but you did not follow?

Why does the LORD lead you into righteousness?

Why does the LORD do things for the purpose of his name?

What is a valley of the shadow of death that you have been in with
the LORD?

Why can we have courage to not fear evil when facing death?

If we shouldn't fear evil, what should we fear?

When in your life have you experienced the presence of the LORD?

What do you think you should do to stay in his presence?

What is an example of the LORD's rod (protection) in your life?

What is an example of the LORD's staff (guidance) in your life?

How can you thank the LORD for his rod and staff?

Have you experienced comfort in the LORD's protection? Explain.

Have you experienced comfort in the LORD's guidance? Explain.

Who are your enemies?

How have you seen the LORD give you a feast before them?

In regards to anointing oil, how has the LORD given respect or honor in your life?

Is there anything in your life that has shown an abundance and overflowing amount of good things?

How has the LORD's goodness followed you in your life?

How has the LORD's unfailing love followed you in your life?

How many days of life are you promised?

What does living in the house of the LORD mean to you?

Does living in the house of the LORD forever sound exciting? Why or why not?

If you could live in the presence of the LORD all day and every day of your life, how would you give thanks?

How can you repay the goodness of the LORD?

How can you repay the lovingkindness of the LORD?

How can you repay the mercy of the LORD?

Do you see this Psalm as positive affirmations, a declaration of your life, or as a prayer?

Do you think David sang this Psalm to God as a prayer?

Other Books by DCE

A Prayer to Our Father in the Heavens: Possibly the Greatest Jewish Prayer of All Time

The Central Tenet of Christianity Found Clearly in the Hebrew Bible: 83 English Translations of Isaiah Chapter 52:13 through Chapter 53

90 English Translations of the Famous Psalm 23 The LORD is my Shepherd

Jesus Resurrects a Dead Girl and Heals a Sick Woman: 124 English Translations of Matthew 9:18-26

Blessed are the…: 121 English Translations of Matthew 5:3-10

The Prophet and Teacher Foretold by Moses is Yeshua (Jesus of Nazareth): 83 English Translations of Deuteronomy 18: 15-19

What Love Is: 124 English Translations of 1 Corinthians 13: 4-7

Jesus Feeds Thousands with Five Loaves of Bread and Two Fish: 124 English Translations of Matthew 14: 15-21

The Golden Rule: 124 English Translations of Matthew 7:12

New Covenant with God Predicted in the Hebrew Bible by the Prophet Jeremiah: 88 English Translations of Jeremiah 31: 31-34

Trust in the LORD with all of Your Heart: 89 English Translations of Proverbs 3: 5-6

Jesus Heals a Paralyzed Man with a Simple Command: 124 English Translations of Matthew 9: 1-8

Importance of Wholehearted and Persistent Prayer and Scriptural Examples of it Causing God to Move and Act on Your Behalf: 124 English Translations of Luke 18: 1-7